Alive By God's Grace
True-Life Adventures of an
African Boy

Levi Makala, PhD, DVM, MBA

Acknowledgements:

To Loretta Emmons for her tireless work rewriting, editing, and illustrating this book I give many thanks. Loretta and I met by circumstances far removed from publishing books, but our kindred spirits seemed to meld the mind and ideas together.

To Loretta's husband Erik Emmons, SPHR, M.S. for his assistance in editing and proofreading the final product many thanks. Also, to my daughters, Ashley and Denise and my wife Clara for assisting with proofreading I thank you. To Ms. Janet Hull much appreciation for being an enthusiastic reader of the book.

Dedication

Thanks to my wife, Clara, for her support and encouragement in all dimensions regarding the need to publish these true stories of my childhood. Without her nudging these would undoubtedly not have been written.

Much credit goes to my daughters, Denise, Ashley and Laura who loved, laughed, appreciated and enjoyed my stories. Their presence and radiance gave me strength to sit down and pen the childhood encounters.

Preface

This book of short stories tells of my mischievous, albeit not purposefully so, childhood growing up in Africa. From lions, to black mamba snakes and all sorts of creatures in between, my life as a boy was not without danger. And through it all, my family and God brought me back from the brink of certain death many times.

It all happened about fifty years ago. I was in elementary school and during this point in my life I was frequently experiencing a mixture of various wonderful and terrifying adventures.

The growing process, as it is called, stretched my imagination and curiosity to the point where only God could intervene and save me from myself.

Not to boast and in all fairness, I was a young, intelligent, studious, pleasant, quintessentially a good lad and adventurous but also very curiously naughty! They say curiosity killed the cat. Well on more than one occasion, it nearly killed me!

I was born in beautiful Zambia. The land of the mighty Victoria Falls, southern Africa.

I had the whole world at my feet. Now I want to share that world with you the reader.

Levi Makala, PhD, DVM, MBA

TABLE OF CONTENTS

Story 1

Levi Learns About the Birds and The Bees

One bright and hot summer day, Levi and his friends went out for a stroll not far from his parents' house. As boys will do, they decided to go bird hunting. It was quite a lot of fun playing bird hunters with [1]catapults (slingshot). The forked sticks with elastic straps were ideal for shooting small stones at their prey. Excitedly the boys filled their pouches with stones that fit the sling shot elastic band. Not too big, not too small. Just the right size for a small hand to send it hurtling through the air.

It was a splendid time of year. The migratory birds were coming in flocks to escape severe weather. The abundant fruits and berries of the region made the perfect place for the birds to settle in and nest.

The young lads were excited. There would be plenty of birds for each boy to hunt. In addition to hunting being great fun, the boys would take the birds home where they were then prepared and eaten by the families. The boys raised their catapults high over their heads and let out wild yells signaling the start of the hunt. With their satchels laden with pebbles and stones steadily slapping their legs, they were off.

---

[1] Malekani or Malegani in Tonga, a forked stick with elastic bands used for hunting small game. Also known as a sling shot.

Levi's mother watched as the boys began their trek to the fruit trees where the birds would likely be eating breakfast. She had warned Levi before his friends arrived to make every effort to stay out of trouble.

"Leave God's creatures alone." She warned him.

Levi nodded and smiled. His curious nature was sometimes overwhelming, but he decided to make every effort to heed her advice. There were so many wonderful sights and fascinating mysteries in the great country of Zambia, and sometimes it was just too much for a small boy to resist the urge to explore.

The lads shouted war cries as they gathered around the [2]Masuku tree. The birds were a flurry of activity flying back and forth, snatching fresh fruit to take back to their nests. The boys pretended to be soldiers and the war was upon them. The birds were the enemy and were stealing the men's rations. The boys whooped again as they readied their catapults.

The tree was in the middle of a field where the land had been cleared for farming.
As is customary, trees with such a good source of food are left standing to provide for the local villages.

---

[2] Masuku tree referred to Uapaca Kirkiana or sugar plum is in the Phyllanthaceae family. This tree is one of the most popular wild fruit trees where eastern Africa meets southern Africa.

The boys were playing under the tree and positioning themselves in spots to hit as many birds as possible. After letting the first shots fly, they noticed there was a whirling mass of bees in the leafy cover of the tree. As they moved around to get a closer look the boys saw a large object hanging from a branch. It was a dark golden giant hive. There was a buzzing clump of insects that enveloped both sides of a branch. A whirling mass of killer [3]bees.

When the boys arrived under the tree to hunt the birds at first, they had not seen the hive. But in very short order, it became apparent the bees were not happy with the intrusion. The boy's stones had narrowly missed the hive, sending bees fluming out of the bottom opening to assess the danger.

The boys moved in for a closer look. This could be a real boon to their day, they decided. A perfect distraction from the mission at hand. Fascinated by the frenzied hive, the boys moved closer to watch as the bees whirled from the branch into the air.

Each boy playfully pushed at the other trying to edge them closer to the hive. They were scared, but the panic made the risk even more appealing to these young boys.

---

[3] These bees are African honey bees known as Nzuki.

Levi could hear his mother's words in his head. "Be careful of the wildlife out there, son, and leave God's creatures alone." Levi chose to ignore these words as the boys stood with their legs apart in a shooter's stance. The boys took perfect aim at the huge hive but were too afraid to shoot. Levi looked at the boy next to him, and then at the next. Each boy looked back momentarily, but then turned to eye the target. The game was on! The oldest boy took the first shot. As the stone smacked the hive part of the swarm billowed out from the bottom. Because the boys could not fully understand the danger their curiosity overruled the possibility that anything would go wrong. Each time a pebble hit the hive, applause erupted from the other boys. The bees, disturbed by the stones, would fly out, and then retreat from the noise as the boys applauded one another.

Each time the bees came too close a yell would ring out, "Take cover guys!" The bees would scout above their heads and then fly back to the hive. With each hit of the target the bees were becoming braver and angrier. It occurred to them that there seemed to be two rather large bees that came closer than the others. They would circle their heads and fly back to the cover of the hive. Levi remembered his father telling him stories about *scout bees*. Scout bees would leave the hive when provoked and circle the enemy. The scouts would then drop a pheromone or scent communicating to the rest of the bees the danger.

The boys jubilantly took turns shooting the hive with their catapults. Levi was a very good shot and had hit the hive more times than his friends. Levi listened to his friends as they urged him to keep shooting. He was pleased to be chosen as the best one for the job and was happy to show off his catapult skills.

As the bee came around again, Levi hesitated. The boys egged him on.

"Come on!" one friend said. "You're not a chicken, are you?"

Another friend joined in the chiding.

"We might get a lot of yummy honey if you can knock it down!"

"Yeah", said another, "prove what a brave soldier you are."

"Don't disturb God's creatures." His mother's warning echoed in his head.

Levi shook his head. He couldn't let his friends think he was afraid. He could do this!

What could go wrong? It was just a bunch of bees.

Levi took aim. "I will be a hero," he thought to himself as he battered the hive over and over. "I will be the champion shooter," he convinced himself as yet another stone hit its mark. "We will all have a sweet treat and they will all thank me," he said to himself. Then he hit the hive again,

And again

And again

And again.

The bee colony shook, and angry bees swarmed out buzzing loudly in protest. The buzzing became closer, louder, and more intense. The boys didn't run at first, as the bees came close, but then circled back to rejoin the rest swarming at the bottom of the hive.

Then something peculiar happened. As Levi let go with one more stone, a lone bee flew overhead and circled him. Quickly the bee left and rejoined the swarm. The boys realized they had pushed the bees into a frenzy.

Suddenly down fell the colony and a black mass of bees came whirling in the boy's direction. Before they knew it, the bees were everywhere. A swarm of what seemed like a thousand angry bees descended on Levi and his accomplices. The boys began running trying to duck for cover and yelping as the bees stung them.

Levi was smaller and although his legs were pumping with all their might, he could not outrun the angry colony of bees. Panting loudly as they ran, the boys zigged this way and that to avoid being stung. There was no admiration for Levi now. He went from hero to zero as the bees stung them all. The only thing the boys could do was run for cover or be stung relentlessly.

As Levi looked left and right, he could not see his playmates as they had all outrun him. He felt the sting of the bees, first at his head and ears, then his arms and body. He began flailing his arms as he continued to try to outrun the angry hoard.

Leaping and jumping around trying to shake off the bees he was now overwhelmed. The entire army of killer African bees engulfed the lad in a stinging frenzy. The bees dive-bombed the poor boy using their stingers like tiny swords pricking and stabbing over and over. Levi called for help, but his friends were already out of ear shot.

Every part of the young boy's body was stung. As he dropped to the ground, there all he could do was curl in a ball and try to become small and invisible. As the lad lay there huddled on the ground taking on a great number of stings, his small body began to react to the venom. Levi shouted to the heavens, "What have I done? I am so sorry bees!" The bees kept stinging his helpless and defenseless body.

His face and limbs began to swell. Bruises marked every sting. The swarm attacked every part of the boy's body covering him from head to toe in a mass of black anger. Already flying into his ears and nose, Levi clamped his lips tight to keep them from entering his mouth.

Levi's parents heard the shouting from the other boys and ran to see what the commotion was all about. They got there very quickly and stood in amazement as the bees suddenly and without warning gathered in a black cloud and returned to their hive. It was as if they had been instructed to leave so the parents could retrieve the child.

Very quickly the venom from hundreds of stings caused Levi to go into shock and eventually cardiac arrest. He was comatose for a week. The doctors told his parents they counted no less than five hundred stings in the boy's body. Levi recalled as he slipped into unconsciousness the words of wisdom his mother had said to him that very morning. Had he heeded her warning he would not be in this predicament.

As Levi waned in and out of coma, thoughts came to him about the events. He felt bad for the bees and the hive. He thought about how he would feel if someone came to his home and beat it down with sticks. He could not blame the bees for defending their home "Leave God's creatures be," resonated in his mind. He did not feel brave. His weapon was no match for the angry bees.

Levi woke in his hospital bed covered in bandages and writhing in pain.

He groaned in agony. The stings felt like a thousand knives poking his body. His parents were at his bedside. The boy's mom and dad reassured him that he was going to be all right. Levi didn't feel like he was going to be alright. He hurt from head to foot. His mother held a cool towel to his small swollen forehead. She shook her head.

"You have been asleep for a week. The boys ran to the house and we rushed you to the hospital." Her voice shook as she spoke, "You were very lucky, Levi." She said with deep concern in her voice.

Levi looked sadly at his mother. "I am so sorry, mom." He said.

His mother nodded. "I know you are, and I believe you have learned a great lesson here. Don't disturb…"

Levi finished her sentence. "God's creatures."

Levi's mother and father told the child, "It is a miracle you have survived and come back to us. "

Levi knew they were right. He knew it was a higher power there with him, watching over him. God had spared his life. It would be weeks before Levi was completely recovered, but once he had recovered there were no real tell-tale signs of the ravage to his body. Levi went about life as usual. He continued to go out with the other boys and hunt and explore. The one thing he never did again was shoot stones at bee hives. He had learned his lesson.

The lesson Levi learned went well beyond not bothering the creatures of Heavenly Father. From that day, he became very compassionate about all of God's creatures and dedicated his life to helping animals. He became a veterinary surgeon and renowned scientist.

Author's Notes

I was lucky to be alive after being viciously attacked by a swarm of killer bees which had been disturbed by noise and attacks from a group of naïve children. My mother and father said it was a miracle that I survived the ordeal. A higher power, the Almighty God was there all the time protecting me from the ordeal. A miracle. It *was* a miracle. God spared my life and I'm thankful." It reminds me of the scripture that states, *"Behold, He that keeps Israel shall neither slumber nor sleep" (Psalms 121:4).*

The doctors said if my mom and my dad had not arrived when they had, I wouldn't have had much longer to live. I was badly swollen and had blisters all over my body. I survived the storm and was kept for observation to ensure all the venom or toxins have been flushed from my system. As in the first days of the Church, God still intervenes today...Supernaturally. He is changing lives for eternity!

My story is about the recovery and the comeback, but I want to make it much more than that. I want to make a positive impact on the world. I am just trying to live each day to the fullest. I want to motivate and hopefully inspire other people through my endeavors to never give up on their dreams. Never stop believing in your faith in God no matter how bad the situation. Everything happens for a reason.

I felt special and loved. I did not have to wait for this tragedy to realize that I mattered to my family and to my Creator. I knew that my life would be spared.

Know that no matter how isolated you may feel, you are never really alone. My parents, relatives and neighbors prayed for me. They earnestly prayed that I would survive and go on to tell others how I made a difference in their life. Believe it or not, I was never scared when I was in this state. I didn't fear death either. When I thought I was dying, I kind of felt at peace. For my family and friends though, this was not the case. They were terrified of losing me. When someone passes away, it is you who is hurting more. My fight to live wasn't for my own life, it was for my mom, dad, brothers and sister's lives.

This near-death experience was indeed a miracle and the life lessons learned through it all cannot be overemphasized. I thought to myself over and over, why this situation had to happen to me. I was always a good kid, received good grades in school, and went to church. Why would something as horrific as this happen to me? Why would God allow this? I went on and on for days asking why? And, then it hit me. All that thinking and pondering on the what-if scenario's and the questionable doubt only stirred up another question – why was I saved? I didn't have any more questions after that. I know what my purpose in life finally is. One cardinal lesson I learned from this experience is that no matter what you do or how you do it and when you do it is not under our control, what is meant to be will be. Really if I was supposed to die, I would have. The doctors thought I was going to die. The odds of surviving a swarm of Killer bee attacks is 1-in-3. I truly verified it. But I survived because it wasn't my time to go. I believe that what is meant to be, will be. Don't stress over trying to control everything in your life! If it is supposed to happen it will.

In retrospect I have experienced that God loves us more than we can ever imagine. There is no question that I learned that God is real and present. He is working in our world. God's miracles are present if we look for them. Heaven is absolutely real. The fact that I am still here on earth to recount this true story is remarkable. Earth or this world is where we learn the lessons, of loving ourselves, loving all beings, showing compassion, forgiveness, acceptance. We are here to do that—manifest every bit of that love and compassion as our souls ascend to higher and higher heights. That's why we are still here on earth. We don't just end this life and go sit in a heaven where there is absolute perfection; this is a dynamic process of learning and growing.

I am so grateful for the miracle of that day. But I feel even more blessed to have that reminder that I must cherish my life and my family's, seize opportunities, enjoy the moments, stop worrying about nonsense and trivialities and invest relentlessly in the most precious relationships of my life. This unforgettable near-death saga gave me perspective that I might never have achieved otherwise. It pushed me off the fence and catapulted me to greater heights.

I Thank God and Praise my God. I also thank my family, especially my mother who stayed with me the entire time at the hospital.

My mother was my constant caregiver and support. I am truly thankful for her vigilant prayers.

Story 2
The Tree of Plenty

The sun was blazing down as the young lads discussed the wild fruit gathering expedition they were about to embark upon. Levi and many of his friends gathered near his home to get the necessary bags and baskets in which to put the ripened delicate fruits. The African Ebony fruit is a green grape-sized fruit which ripens to a lovely golden yellow color. This fruit ripens during the dry season, which makes it even more important for the region. God had laid out a perfect scenario for the Tonga region. Some vegetation was available in abundance in the rainy season, while others like the Ebony fruit were ready in the dry season. So, each season had its offerings for the table and for sales at small impromptu roadside markets. These small stands were set up at the end of the picking day and taken down at dusk.

The six boys, Paul, Crispin, Lambwe, Haiten, Lodo, and Levi, followed by Lambwe's four dogs, journeyed to the large dark barked tree to pick fruit. As was customary for the area, the boys had to leave very early in the morning, so they could pick fruit without competing with wild baboons and other animals.

The dogs ambled along with the boys. The Jack Russel was quite adventurous and would bound about chasing small rodents as they neared the tree. The boys and their parents felt safer when the boys were accompanied by the dogs. The German Shepherds were natural protectors and would bark a warning if anything was awry. Unfortunately, they also barked excitedly as the Jack Russel scurried about chasing varmints.

The boys laughed out loud at the antics of the dogs. Every now and then Lambwe would whistle to the dogs to keep them close. They would run from all directions to join the boys until the next chase was on. The walk to the main tree was long. The tree stood in massive glory in the middle of a corn field. When fruit bearing trees are found growing on farmland, they are never cut, but left to grow and provide much needed food for the villages. This tree had been in the middle of the corn field for many years and had grown strong and healthy. It always provided the greatest amount and juiciest fruits of all the Black Ebony, sometimes referred to as Jackal Berry, trees. The fruit was very similar to the persimmon in shape, color and taste. The boys were excited as they traversed the five-mile dusty road to the tree.

Once the tree was spotted, the boys let out a simultaneous whoop of delight to signal the mad dash to the tree to get the best branch to perch upon for fruit harvesting. They raced quickly with the dogs keeping pace.

As each boy settled onto a branch, Levi chose a forked branch. This made picking fruit in all directions very easy because it was like being cradled in a chair. The older boys had decided to climb higher to retrieve the largest number of fruits the tree had to offer.

The dog's tongues lolled out of their mouths and they rested in the shade of the tree. Every now and then the Jack Russell would race off after some unseen trespasser. As the boys filled their containers with berries, they did so with great speed. They knew once the bags and wicker wood baskets were full, they could enjoy the spoils of their journey and eat some of the fruits themselves.

The boys sat back to enjoy the delicious fruits when the larger dogs began barking. By instinct the boys looked out across the field to make sure there were no baboons or jackals headed toward the tree. Satisfied that the dogs were just egging on the Jack Russel, they settled back down to enjoy their snack.

The large dogs continued to bark, and Levi shouted up to his friends, "Guys, we need to be looking around. The dogs are barking a lot. Maybe they see something in the distance we can't see yet."

The lads higher in the tree gave Levi a thumbs up. They put their hand on their brow above their eyes to block out the sun and squinted to look as far as they could across the corn field. Paul called down to Levi, "All clear!" Levi relaxed. He decided that the dogs just wanted attention. He laughed at the silliness and settled back into the arm of the tree.

Sitting straddling a tree branch can become uncomfortable, and Levi decided to adjust his seat on the limb. He placed his hand on the branch between his legs to wriggle his body into a more comfortable position. The branch felt odd. It was soft under the touch. Squishy, almost. His small hand squeezed a time or two while his mind was trying to make sense of a warm and pliable branch. It was at that moment that Levi realized he was sitting, not on a branch made of bark and wood, but on the body of a very large snake.

Attempting not to scream, he released his grip on the snake's body only to find himself face to face with a mighty King Cobra. The snake had turned the front half of its body, so the head was facing the frightened boy. It flicked an angry tongue at the boy and reared its head up in warning. The small boy could not move off the snake fast enough and the mighty reptile spread its massive head and neck creating the distinctive hood of a cobra. The snake showed its fangs and began to rear its head back as if to strike. The whole time the snake's body was angrily trying to slither itself from under the boy.

The boys realized now why the dogs had been barking so incessantly. They had seen the snake and tried to warn the boys of the danger. Levi, in a moment of desperation yelled out, "KING COBRA IN THE TREE!" As he yelled he let go of the branch and threw himself from the tree. The other boys had already begun jumping to the ground. The ploughed ground beneath was soft, but a fall from 20 feet or more could have proven fatal.

The older boys were further out on their limbs and were able to easily jump to safety. However, Levi was nestled in the center of the tall tree, and his fall to freedom was much more painful as he hit branch after branch on his way down. Thud! He landed hard. Fear overcame any pain and the boys hoisted their bags and baskets up and ran as fast as they could away from the tree. It is not uncommon for an angry cobra to chase its prey. The boys were relieved to see the snake still lounging in the tree when they had gotten some distance away. The snake could have struck long before Levi realized that was what he was seated upon. The Lord protected Levi by allowing the snake to give a warning before striking. That warning saved Levi's life.

Author's Notes:

As a lad I thought, "Even a poisonous cobra, who doesn't bite or harm anyone, is given the name 'good'. By the hand of God, I lived to tell the tale. Believe it or not…I lost all fear of snakes!

And now as an adult, the lessons from my childhood King Cobra encounter still speak to me today! The fact that I am here to recount this event is more a tribute not to luck or good judgement but protection from a higher power, The Almighty God.

There are many reasons I am thankful of a good outcome with a Cobra at such a close distance. I learned to be ever diligent and aware of my surroundings. Through these experiences I have come to develop a strong sense of the smell of snakes.

I can tell just by smell if a snake is in close proximity. That snake would have killed me if I had not taken the initiative to let go of the branch and jump to the ground. God saved my life!

Some words of wisdom. If or when you encounter a King Cobra don't panic, they are timid and as frightened of you, as you are of them! Be alert at all times when in the bush, especially in the early morning during the warmer months when snakes are more likely to be sunning themselves but are slow to react. Wear shoes and trousers, instead of sandals and shorts.

These simple things may be the difference between living to tell the tale and becoming a snake bite statistic.

Story 3

Braving the Zambezi River

The Zambezi River also known as the "river of life" flows through six countries including Zambia. It is there that this adventure took place.

From the time of his youth, Levi and his friends would trek to the cool clean waters of the Zambezi River to explore and sit in the white sands of the shore. The walk to the river was long and hot, and the boys often cooled themselves at the river's edge. The older boys who knew how to swim dove in and enjoyed water games and races. Levi had not yet learned to swim and was not allowed to go to the river unattended.

On a hot October morning Andrew and George, longtime friends of Levi and his family, invited Levi to the river to watch the hippos and various fish and wildlife. Levi never passed up the opportunity to go to the river and excitedly told his mother where he was going.

As was always customary, a child never left the safety of home without telling a parent or other adult where they would be. In Africa one must always be aware of lions, crocodiles, hippos and other dangers.

As Levi started to leave, his mother reminded him,

"Do not stray from the older boys. If you fall in, call for help, but don't thrash about. Stay calm. Don't go into the deep waters. The current is swift, and you could be swept away."

Levi nodded impatiently. He knew his mother was worried about him going to the river, but he heard the lecture every time he went to play near the Zambezi.

Andrew and George had gathered a small army of children to go swimming. They were the oldest and were expected to keep a keen eye on the children who had not yet learned to swim. Levi was among those who had not mastered the art of staying afloat in the water.

As they trekked toward the river, Levi was more and more determined to learn to swim. He wanted to be one of the "on duty" kids who helped the others stay safe. The parade of lads walked the long distance to the river. It took nearly an hour to get there. By the time they arrived any worries about the rushing waters, hippos, and such had vanished. They were hot and sweaty and ready to cool off. The boys threw their clothes on the sand and headed to the water. Swimming in the nude was always fun and seemed far more natural than trying to stay afloat in water laden garments.

The beautiful spring fed river meandered lazily by.

"It doesn't seem so bad", Levi thought to himself. Levi looked around at the beauty surrounding them. Impressive rock formations and lavish vegetation seemed to lull Levi into a spell. He forgot about the challenges of learning to swim as he admired the nature surrounding them.

Children of Levi's age generally waded in the shallow waters until someone took the time to teach them the basics of swimming. George and Andrew were anxious to dive in and cool off, so they gave the children simple swimming and lifesaving instructions. They were told to obey all the rules and to avoid wandering away from the group.

The youngster's faces were skewed in tight lipped angst as they tried to understand the quick swimming lesson. "Hold your breath, put your body flat in the water, don't dive until you can paddle a little on top, stay near the shore, if you get in trouble call out for help, if someone else is in trouble go to them and help them to shore." It was all said so fast and back and forth between the two boys that it was confusing. However, Levi was not about to miss the opportunity to learn to swim.

The older boys' instructions stuck in his head as he inched his way into the water. Levi stretched his arms out in front of him as if he might attempt a dive. He thought better of it and decided to try a simple float first. He eased his body forward, legs out behind him, gently lifting off the river bed as he had seen the older boys do many times. In a flash the water of the river was over his head as he sunk! Levi stood up, shook his head and tried to float again and again. He could not stay on top of the water. He was in barely knee-deep water and decided that the problem must be there was not enough water to keep him buoyant. Dismissing the rules laid out by the older kids, Levi moved into deeper water.

Now chest deep in the water, Levi lurched forward, arms outstretched, and sunk! As he struggled to get his feet beneath him, he realized quickly that he had been carried by the current to a distance that was too deep for him to stand. As he attempted to get to the surface his mind let go of the training and he thrashed excitedly trying to get air. He felt the river lapping at him. It was rocking him up and down and back and forth at the same time. Levi lost all sense of direction. As the current continued to sweep him away he was pulled into a hole where he swirled about. He could not take in any air.

"This is it," he thought, "I am going to die." His stomach had filled with water and there was no room left to breath. Just as he began to sink into the depths of the pool dragging him under, he saw a hand above him. In one final attempt he reached up toward it. Perhaps he was dreaming. Perhaps it was just hoping that made him think he saw help arriving. He sunk into unconsciousness.

Fortunately, by the grace of God, an older boy had snagged his small outstretched hand and plucked the boy from the river. It was Andrew and George. They had seen Levi trying to swim and watched in horror as he sunk and disappeared beneath the current. The boys dragged the limp body to shore. There was yelling and chaos. The smaller children were told to get out of the water until the emergency was over. Some of the smaller children were crying looking at Levi's lifeless body.

Andrew knelt beside the boy and began pushing hard on his chest and stomach. George was watching the other children to make certain all were accounted for. Andrew looked up at George in panic and then to the heavens. "Please God," he begged. "Please bring him back." He pressed a good hard push and a spout of water erupted from Levi's mouth. Levi whimpered slightly, and Andrew pushed again. This time more water and an awful gagging sound came from Levi. Levi's eyes opened, and Andrew cheered.

The smaller children gathered closer to see the miracle as Levi stood on rubbery legs. They offered to help the boy as they gathered their clothes for the long walk back home.

The ashen faces of the children told a story of something awry, and although Levi was feeling fine when they arrived home, he was scolded for not heeding the rules. His parents were very grateful that he was fine. They knew that most children learning to swim intake some water. They were not fully aware of how close he had come to drowning that day.

A few weeks passed, and the boys came again to ask if Levi wanted to go to the Zambezi for a swim. Levi accepted with great enthusiasm. He was more determined than ever to learn to swim properly. When they arrived, he asked the older boys to watch over him while he attempted to swim. They nodded and each one took a stance on either side of him.

Levi put his hands on the bottom of the river in shallow water. He kicked his legs up and down, practicing his movement. He nodded at the older boys and headed into deeper water. When he could barely keep his feet flat on the ground, he sprung up and out. He felt himself sinking slightly so he inhaled deeply. His body rose to the surface and he was floating. This was one of the most exciting feelings he had ever had. He exhaled and started to feel his body sink. He inhaled and up came his body. He had it! Now he began slowly kicking his feet. He felt himself propelling in the water.

"Hey, Levi," Andrew called, "Turn back this way. Don't get too far from shore."

George was so excited all he could do was whoop, "He's doing it! He's swimming!"

Levi was doing it. He was swimming. This was the beginning of many years of enjoying the cool waters of the Zambezi River.

Author's Notes

The experience of near drowning left me completely changed. I became a born-again Christian and decided to use my own experiences to help others. The Lord God Almighty allowed me to have such an experience as part of my growth. I could not see God during the event, yet I could somehow sense He was winking at me. It was as if He was letting me know it would be all right.

He had shown me evidence of His fatherly love and caring. He seemed to be letting me know that life here on earth is but a blink of the eye. Heaven is a vision that spans eternity. We are all special in God's eyes. Whether we ask for His help or not, He is there to protect and save us. He is good to everyone. The bad, the good, and the ugly. He is loving and compassionate and impartial. I pray people learn that He is always faithful to us. No matter how tough things get, He is always with us.

Today I spend much of my time counseling the hurting, dying and grieving.

I thank and praise God that I am alive to be able to help others.

Story 4

The Attack of the Black Mamba

Boys will be boys. In Africa that adage carries a whole different set of circumstances than most any place else in the world. Boys will be boys. When they see lions in the distance, boys will be boys. When they are attracted to slithery moving snakes in the jungles, and then set out to trap those snakes, yes, unfortunately, boys will be boys.

The large tree behind Levi's house was easy to climb and gave an excellent vantage point to the surrounding area. Beneath the tree was an old dilapidated latrine. The walls had fallen in and the roof collapsed from neglect and vandalism. From the tree one could see into the pit of the latrine quite well.

The tree was a veritable playground for Levi and the neighboring children. They had seen baboons jump from limb to limb with great ease. The children decided it would be exciting to do the same. Pretending to be monkeys, they leapt from this branch to that. This was a game they played over and over.

As Levi climbed the tall tree on that particular morning, he stopped midway to have a good look into the latrine pit. He narrowed his eyes against the afternoon sun and looked hard. Nothing new or exciting. Then he went about swinging from limb to limb. He climbed down the tree and thought he had seen something move inside the fallen building. Although there had been many mice and bugs and even lizards taking cover in the broken-down building, this movement was somehow different. There was no scurrying sound or quick sharp movements. This was slow and methodical. Levi thought he should have a closer look.

Once again, he climbed the tree, this time perching on a branch just above the wrecked outhouse. Much to his horror, Levi saw a snake slither from one end of the privy to the other. Not knowing what kind of snake, it was, Levi was relieved that he had climbed the tree to look. Pit vipers, cobras and other poisonous and dangerous snakes are indigenous to Zambia. It could have been a fatal mistake to have looked in the latrine from the ground. The snake was relatively small, so Levi was not sure what species it was.

Levi exited the tree and slowly moved away from the latrine. He needed to find more boys to help capture or kill it. He shouted, "Mom, there's a [4]snake in the old latrine!" His mother raced to meet him.

"A snake?" she asked with concern.

"Yes, in the latrine. A black snake. I will show you." Levi took his mother's hand and led her to the latrine. Because the children spent so much time in the big tree, his mother didn't really believe there was a snake. But she had to be certain.

Levi's friends had heard him hollering to his mother. They all came clamoring to see what the excitement was about. As they approached the opening of the dwelling, the snake lay quietly basking itself in the sunshine at the opening of the pit. With a stick, Levi's mother prodded the snake to see if it was alive. It slithered into the pit. Levi's mother jumped and let out a yelp as though she had been attacked. The children giggled at her reaction. Levi pointed to the place where the snake retreated, and his mother made her way closer. The snake poked its head out again causing her to shriek one more time. Levi took a whack at the snake with his stick, and the snake disappeared once more.

Snakes in the region of Zambia usually survive on rats and mice and other small rodents. But a snake that is quite hungry will attack small children. For that reason, a snake living so close to the family dwelling had to be dealt with quickly. The boys decided the best way to rid the neighborhood of the snake was to use glass from broken bottles and from the latrine as a trap. In their naivete the boys assumed the snake would crawl across the glass, cutting itself to smithereens. They spent an afternoon shattering glass bottles and

---

[4] Nzoka isiya (black snake)

being careful not to disturb the snake, pressed the glass into the ground leaving very sharp edges poking skyward. The boys had a great time setting the trap for the snake.

Months passed and there was no sign that the snake had crossed the shards of glass. The children forgot all about the trap and the snake as they continued to mimic the monkeys in the tall tree. Climbing higher and higher and leaping further and further, they were becoming quite good at limb jumping.

One morning the boys climbed the tree and after about an hour of leaping from this limb to that, the boys decided to rest. As the branches on the tree were quite large, the boys decided to stretch out on various branches and take a needed break. Levi chose the big branch that stretched out over the abandoned latrine. Just as he was settling down on the branch something caught his eye. He did a double take. He had not expected to see something moving down below, but lo and behold, there it was, the snake! Only this time the snake was very large. It had grown to nearly nine feet long with a very wide body. The snake was flicking its tongue as it looked up the tree. Suddenly it began to climb the tree. It was moving very quickly, and Levi yelled to his companions. "SNAKE!"

The boys became panic stricken. They were far up in the tree and the snake was blocking the only exit. The boys began leaping from the tree. They landed safely, yelling loudly, "Snake! There is a snake in the tree!"

Levi looked down and realized he was on the only branch that hung out over the latrine and all the broken glass still protruding from the ground. Levi began screaming at the snake. As it reached the same branch Levi was perched on, he jumped up and down trying to shake the snake onto the ground.

The snake paid no attention to the small boy's frantic actions. Levi moved further away from the trunk of the tree. The branch began to bend under his weight. The snake slithered onto the branch. It didn't matter if the snake was mad or hungry. The only thing that mattered was that Levi had to stay away from it. As he inched himself further out on the limb, it gave way.

CRACK! Down fell Levi and half the branch. Down onto the broken glass bottles. They tore at his skin and clothing. Blood gushed from his head and body as the glass cut him all over.

Levi attempted to stand but fell heavily to the ground. He had broken his leg and an arm in the fall. The boys were yelling for help and trying not to panic over their bloody friend laying on the glass-littered ground.

Neighbors came running to see the snake reach the bottom of the tree and glide toward the fallen lad. Swiftly they attacked the snake with sticks and shovels. The snake stopped a mere few feet from the boy. Levi's mother ran toward her son.

"Make sure that snake is dead." She yelled as she gathered Levi in her arms. A neighbor helped his mother carry him to the side of the house where they painstakingly removed glass from his body and face. They rushed him to the hospital. Levi survived another ordeal that would prove to make him stronger and more devoted to God. With his family's love and support he made a full recovery.

Author's Notes

I was comforted by how much my parents worried about me. What a great family I had! I'm so thankful to the Almighty God for yet another miracle. He was there all the time to rescue me.

There have been many people during my childhood years who were supportive and compassionate. Friends, family, and colleagues. But I literally wouldn't be here if it weren't for my brave and supportive parents and neighbors who risked their lives saving mine in the hour of need. For that and for them I am infinitely grateful.

We don't always understand why things happen the way they do. God is sovereign and can do what He wants to do, whenever He wants to do it. He is omniscient and knows everything. Therefore, when you suffer a loss, hurt or tragedy, you must understand that the Almighty God knows things about the situation at hand to which you have not been made privy.

Therefore, when you don't understand what God is doing, you must trust in Him. He loves you and has your best interests at heart. This traumatic scenario will be indelibly etched into my memory for eternity as I have seen and tasted of the goodness of the Lord. Even if I had not committed my life at that tender age, He was there all the time for me, just in time to rescue me. He is there and will be there for you too.

Story 5

The Mushroom, the Lion and the Boy

Growing up in rural Zambia there were many adventures for a young lad. However, as infants, children were carried in a [5]satchel on their mother's back. This would seem to be the safest place of all. Levi was very small and still being carried by his mother as she went about her chores.

The rainy season was a time of mushroom gathering in Zambia. Mushrooms were in high season then, and a great source of both food as well as income to the locals. The women gathered their wickerwork baskets and headed to the fields to forage for the edible fungus. Many of the women carried their children while gathering. December was the principal month when mushrooms peaked in abundance and diverse variety.

Levi's mother, Ms. Estelle and several village women gathered to plan out the morning harvesting. Judith, Jocelyn, and Molly all relied on the wisdom of the elder women, Ms. Estelle, Jelinah and Elizabeth to direct the picking of the mushrooms. Because the mushrooms were a delicacy and hard to see, it was imperative that they moved slowly in a deliberate line to reap the best possible harvest and leave no mushroom behind. The women hoisted their small children onto their backs and began the walk to the

---

[5] Chitenge was a large piece of cloth which was wrapped around mother and baby, so the woman could work while carrying the child.

forest area where the mushrooms were in abundance. The children swayed back and forth in rhythm with the women's hips and fell asleep against their mother's backs almost immediately.

The women agreed on a location where they had great success picking mushrooms in past years. They began the tedious inch- by- inch movement while scanning ahead with their eyes. Once a small patch of mushrooms was found, the women knew they were in a good spot to continue. The sun in the early morning to midmorning was best for mushroom hunting. But in the heat of the day, the blazing sun became almost unbearable. The women decided to stop and seek shade under a small grove of trees.

As the women began to set their baskets down, Elizabeth felt a tingle along her neck. She looked at Ms. Estelle, and said, "Do you feel something odd here?"

Ms. Estelle looked about. At first, she was going to wave off Elizabeth's notion that it was unsafe to rest in the shade of the trees. Just as she was about to shake her head a wave of uneasiness came over her as well. The unmistakable rising of the hair on the back of her neck told Ms. Estelle that something was amiss. She looked about uneasily. They had continued walking toward the trees, when movement caught their eyes. There in the same shade they so desperately wanted was a pride of lions taking full advantage of the coolness under the trees. The women inhaled deeply trying not to panic. They wanted to scream but knew that would mean an attack. They looked at each other and with a simultaneously understanding nod, took a slow step backwards. Their only hope of not being seen was to move in unison and quietly. They seemed to all be holding their breaths. Inch by inch they moved away from the tree.

Slowly the women continued walking backwards never taking their eyes off the lions. The lions were very lazy, and no doubt had full stomachs, or they would certainly have attacked immediately. They didn't seem to notice the panic-stricken women who were gingerly making their way back toward the path to town.

Once the women felt they were a safe distance from the beasts of the jungle, they dropped their wickerwork baskets and ran as fast as they could toward town. In such a panic were the women that when Levi's satchel came loose, and he fell to the ground, his mother did not notice. When the women reached town, screaming to the townsfolk, "There are lions in the forest!" People came running. Ms. Estelle reached for the satchel strap to remove Levi from her back only to realize in that instant that the child and the cloth were missing. Ms. Estelle became hysterical with fright.

"My baby has been eaten by a pride of lions!" she wailed. Onlookers tried to calm her to no avail. She looked at her companions. Their eyes widened as they realized she wanted to go back and look for her son. The women shook their heads frantically. They had been frightened enough for one day. Besides, what good would it do? If the lions indeed had taken the child, there would be nothing left to find. They cast their eyes to the ground still shaking their heads.

Ms. Estelle could not go home and tell her husband, Silas, that she had dropped their son and lions had eaten him. She had to know for sure before taking the news home.

In a flash she began tracing her steps along the trail. She left the path headed toward the woodland area where the mushrooms grow. In the distance she saw the stand of trees where the women sought shade. She moved cautiously toward the trees. She heard a sound and turned her head to listen intently. There it was again. A whimper. She held her breath. Could it be?

She moved swiftly toward the sound and there, sitting in the tall grass, crying, was Levi.

Ms. Estelle scooped him into her arms and hoisted him onto her hip. She grabbed the cloth from the ground and steadily moved back to the path. She was very emotional but knew she had to keep calm and just move along to safety. She did not see the lions under the trees, but since they tend to blend into the scenery, she could not take any chances. Once on the main road back to town, Ms. Estelle took a moment to make sure Levi was all right. She hugged him tightly and a tear of relief rolled down her face.

The townsmen came armed to defend the woman and child. She told them that the lions had moved on. They went to the stance of trees and found clear evidence of a large pride of lions. It is unusual for a pride to move in so close to a village. This made the men nervous, so they hunted for the lions for several hours. The lions had no doubt been frightened away by the women as they tore down the road screaming, "Lions, lions in the forest!"

Author's Notes:

It must have been by the grace of God that this apparent miracle happened. In retrospect this incidence reminds me of the three men in the den of lions in the book of Daniel. The lions did not harm them because God had protected them.

After a disturbing and hair-raising encounter with a pride of lions, I counted my blessings. An infant left alone near a pride of lions, even those who have already fed, is a sure recipe for disaster. Like the three men in the den of lions, the lions could not even come near me. I am clear about one thing – had it not been for the Almighty God's mercy, compassion and protection, I would not have been around to tell my story. In retrospect, I can see how God saved my life by quieting me until I heard my mother approaching. Then the slightest whimper, as though He were helping me stay calm, led my mother to me.

Story 6

A Thorny Thicket Teaches a Lesson

Levi jumped out of bed in the wee hours of the morning. He wanted to go bird hunting. As he quietly closed the door behind him, his younger sister, Eunice slid out beside him. Levi wrinkled his nose. He did not want to be bothered looking after his sister. He knew if he made a fuss about it, he may not be allowed to go hunting. He sighed deeply and motioned for her to return to the house. In the past Levi had always tried to avoid taking his sister with him. She slowed him down. Eunice was always chasing after butterflies or talking incessantly. Levi's mother, Ms. Estelle stepped outside as Eunice began to fret about being left behind. She tried to talk to Levi, but he would not budge. Not this time.

Ms. Estelle shook her head and motioned for Eunice to come back into the house. She knew once her son made up his mind, he was not going to back down. Besides there were things Eunice could help her with in the home. She smiled at Levi as he gathered his slingshot and stones and moved toward the thorny thicket about four hundred yards from their home.

Levi strolled along the gravel road. A dole of doves flew past him and into the thicket. Although the thorny bushes were thick with barbs, the boys had managed to penetrate it successfully. It wasn't easy, but it paid off. Inside the brush one could be part of the scenery and bird hunting became very easy. While the birds hunted insects hiding in the shrubbery, Levi hunted the birds.

This particular thicket was a favorite place for many birds including quail. There were always dangers when weaving into the thorny branches. Becoming stuck or shredding oneself on the thorns was a constant danger. Venomous snakes and other animals made the thorny hedge their home. But none of that mattered to Levi as he hunted the birds. He was quite an adept hunter. He knew when to move deeper into the bushes, and when to hold his position for a good solid shot.

Levi's aim was true as he shot one then two then three birds. He used a small stick to pull them close then picked them up and put them in his bag. Today was a good hunting day and Levi had bagged several birds when he felt a strange tingly sensation above his ear. He froze. Levi felt as though his hair was raising on his head.

"What is that?" he wondered. "Is that a ghost touching me?" He looked around to make certain it wasn't his pesky sister or one of his friends playing a prank on him. No one was there. As he stood waiting to see what was going to happen the urge to look up overcame him. There, about nine feet above his head was a six-foot Black Mamba snake watching him with a great deal of interest.

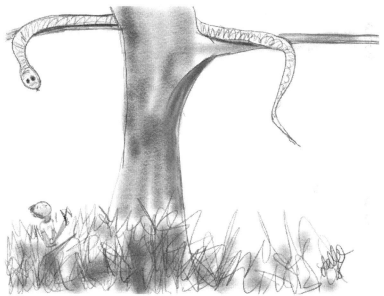

In Zambia, as in all of Africa, snakes abound throughout the region. There are poisonous snakes, such as cobras, mambas, and common non-poisonous snakes like the python. Knowing which snakes to avoid can save lives. One of the more elusive but highly venomous snakes is the Black Mamba. The snake is not actually black but takes its name from the black interior of its mouth. At ten years old, Levi had little experience with large venomous snakes. He had been schooled on which ones to avoid, and how to move slowly away when one encounters such a snake. But, herein was the predicament: how in the world was he going to slowly back away from a snake directly above him in a patch of thorns so thick it took him a half an hour to penetrate? Levi knew he was within striking distance of the huge snake. It must have been watching him hunt. Perhaps it wanted to grab one of the fallen birds, thus making its hunt easier. Levi gathered his bag of birds, dropped the stone from his slingshot into the bag and took one deft step backwards. His foot found ground beneath and he raised his other leg and placed his foot behind the other. His eyes never left the snake. The big snake lay on the branch. Every now and then a flick of the tongue as if testing the air could be seen by the boy.

Levi didn't worry about the thorns. Although it took Levi a long time to enter the bramble, miraculously he managed to evade the snake and exit in less than five minutes. He was scratched as he moved backward step after step. His arms were bleeding, and thorns were stuck in his clothes. Once out of the thicket he ran straight home to tell the tale of the giant Black Mamba in the thorny bushes. His mother knew he was telling the truth. She was also glad that his sister had stayed home after all.

A few minor scratches were nothing compared to what could have happened in the thicket on that cool summer morning.

Author's Notes

The Black Mamba **(Dendroaspis polylepis)**, is one of Africa's most feared and respected snakes. The mere mention of the snake can invoke fear, respect or awe. It was once believed that if bitten by a Black Mamba the end came quickly.

The Black Mamba is named for the color of the inside of its mouth. This is clearly displayed when it is threatened. Its preferred habitat includes termite mounds, hollow tree trunks, and moist savannah and lowland tropical forests.

The snake is not aggressive and will do anything in its power to move away from humans rather than attack. Mambas are feared through much of Africa for their speed, aggressiveness and deadly venomous bites. Their genus name, Dendroaspis, means "tree snake." Most mambas spend much of their time in trees. Black Mambas can be very aggressive when cornered.

After a disturbing and hair-raising encounter with a six-foot-long Black Mamba, I counted my blessings as I could have been bitten by the snake and would have died.

I am clear about one thing – had it not been for the Almighty Gods mercy, compassion and protection, I would not have been around to tell my story. In retrospect, I can see how God saved my life, and made sure I got out of the thorny bush thicket in a remarkable five minutes.

Story 7

The Prodigy Snake Charmers

Peanut farming in Zambia is huge business and keeps hundreds of thousands of peasants in the fields cultivating the crop. Peanuts are a modest means of support for many families in Zambia. They provided food as well as some additional income with which to support the family.

Ms. Estelle, Levi's mother, had a small patch of ground she worked by hand to plant and harvest the ground nuts. The walk to the field was two miles, so with her hoe in one hand and Levi on her hip, she trudged to the field every morning

As Ms. Estelle set out that warm summer morning her youngest daughter Eunice was in a satchel on her back, and Levi was being carried on her hip. It was common for the women to tend the fields while caretaking the smallest children. Ms. Estelle untied the sling that carried the girl, she placed the two children on the cloth under a tree to rest, and then set to work. The children played happily in the dirt.

Planting and caring for the peanut plants cannot be done in a day. So, each day, she would follow the routine, taking the children along with her. Although the field wasn't large by farming standards, it was quite a task for one person to harvest. Ms. Estelle began the arduous task of pulling up the plants, testing a few pods to be sure they were ready for harvest, and then digging and piling each bush. Picking peanuts is a multi-step process. One must dig the plant from the ground, cutting the tap root in the process. Then the dirt is shaken from the plant, and the plant is placed inverted, so the nuts are exposed to the sun for drying. This process is backbreaking and takes a skilled hand. She worked diligently while the children played.

A lone tree in the middle of the field provided shade for the youngsters while they played. But after some time in the heat, they fell asleep. Ms. Estelle looked up from time to time to check on the children. When she noticed they were asleep, she went to them and placed the chitenge cloth over them. She went back to the field happy knowing the children were sleeping soundly and safe from the sun's hot rays.

Ms. Estelle was engrossed in harvesting. She straightened up, stretching her tired back, and looked in the direction of the children. She squinted against the sun. She could see the children were awake. It appeared they were playing with something. She put her hand over her brow to get a better look.

Whatever they were playing with, seemed to be moving back and forth. As the children stood and hopped and swayed about, so did the object in front of them.

Ms. Estelle felt an uneasiness come over her. "Surely this is not a snake", she thought. She watched a few more moments as Eunice chattered away trying to touch the moving object. As she tried to touch it one more time, Ms. Estelle realized whatever it was had been dodging the children's grasp.

Ms. Estelle knew at that moment it was a snake! A very large snake. It was reared up holding its huge head above the children and swaying to and fro as the children moved back and forth in front of it. Ms. Estelle knew she could not go to the children. The snake apparently did not feel threatened by the children and seemed to be enjoying the game. Levi would try to grab the snake's tail, and it would coil it up tighter to its body. Eunice wanted to touch its head. She attempted on several occasions to grab the snake's long neck. While Ms. Estelle watched in horror, she called out to women from the neighboring fields. They came quickly to see what the commotion was all about. Each was more shocked than the last.

Twice Ms. Estelle seemed to grow weak in the knees, nearly passing out from the fear of the events unfolding before her eyes. The women gathered around her, reassuring her. They shook their heads and held her arms when she would try to go to the children's aid. Any approach by an adult, or someone seemingly a threat and the snake could become defensive and strike. Ms. Estelle dropped to her knees, clasped her hands together, and began to pray to the Lord for the children's safety.

The women argued quietly amongst themselves as to the species of snake. Some thought it was a python, while others said it was a grass snake. The one thing that was certain, it was large enough to have devoured one or both of the children. Most children don't survive an interchange of this nature. Snakes, although not predatory to humans by nature, will most often strike when provoked. It was quite obvious as the children chattered and giggled, reaching for the snake over and over that for all intents and purposes, this snake was being provoked.

Ms. Estelle rose from the ground and watched as the snake dance continued for what seemed an eternity. Just as she and the other women were formulating a plan and grabbed sticks from the ground, the snake dropped to the ground and slithered away. It slithered right past the women, over the peanut mounds and into the forest. The women raised their sticks as if to warn the snake to keep moving. As it slithered into the forest, Ms. Estelle raced to her children. She scooped them into her arms and praised the Lord for their safety. The women gathered around regaling the impossible story that they would have to tell their families when they returned home that evening.

Author's Note:
My mother, Ms. Estelle, counted her blessings and thanked the Almighty God for sparing her children from danger. In retrospect, I see God's mighty hand over my life. He has been faithful and showed mercy to me and kept me safe.

Story 8
Boys, Bicycles, and Baboons

Bicycling is one of the most basic modes of transportation in Zambia. For young boys it's the most fun and rewarding, so boys learn to ride adult bikes at a very early age. Levi and his friends all learned to ride two wheelers by the time they were seven years old.

Learning to ride a bike was not easy in Zambia. There were no sidewalks, so the boys learned to ride on a soccer field. The bicycle offered freedom to the boys who would otherwise have to walk everywhere. It didn't matter the terrain, gravel, sand, mud, it was always exhilarating. Levi and his brother Kenny each had bikes handed down from their father. They were the perfect size and the boys could easily straddle the bikes and place their feet firmly on the ground on either side. Bikes in Zambia were somewhat different than bikes in other parts of the world. These bikes had no hand brakes. Instead, they were designed to stop when the boys pedaled backwards very quickly until the brake engaged. In extreme situations, this could lead to wipe outs, or bypassing a turn.

Kenny and Levi rode their bikes everywhere. They rode them to school, to the neighborhood shops, to the river, and to their friend's homes. It was the best and most fun form of transportation according to the boys.

When Levi was entering the sixth grade he and his friends would ride their bikes on a long trek to the water treatment tanks. The tanks were located on a tall hill and riding down toward town was great fun. They would reach very fast speeds and peddle frantically backwards to brake before crashing into a tree or missing the road at the bottom of the hill. On this summer day, the road had been graded and the ride was smooth as can be. Each boy walked their bikes up the steep hill. They would then mount the bikes and let gravity and the steep slope take over, barreling down the hill. It was exciting.

The boys walked the bikes up, sped down the hill, and walked up again for three rotations that day. The boys met up and rode the hill for three consecutive days. Then on that fateful summer day, Levi found himself going alone. His friends were unable to go with him, so he made the trek to the water treatment area by himself. He walked up the hill, he said a prayer for safety, planted the bike on the gravel trail, straddled the frame and inhaled a deep breath. He pushed off, let out a mighty "Whoop!" and was racing down the hill.

Somewhere about half way down the hill, his bike hit a small bunch of gravel which propelled Levi into a tree. It did not stop his bike as he bounced off the tree and seemed to pick up even greater speed. Levi was scared but excited. However, his excitement turned to dread as he realized he was about to run head long into another kind of obstacle all together.

Baboons are free roaming bands of monkeys found in all regions of Africa. They are large and travel in groups. They are ground dwellers and move about at all different times of the day and evenings. Not particularly aggressive, they can become protective of their babies when threatened. The congress of baboons in front of Levi's fast-moving bicycle seemed disinterested in the oncoming danger. They had camped out in the middle of the roadway and were not moving out of his way. Levi let out a yell" Get out of the way! Get out of the way!" But the Baboons just watched as the bicycle flew down the hill toward them. The baby monkeys clung to their mother's backs and watched as the boy got closer and closer.

Levi pedaled backward with all his power. His bike did not respond. No brake engaged. Levi did the only thing he could do to avoid hitting the troupe of Baboons. He flung himself sideways and crashed to the ground. Pain covered his small body. His left hand was driven hard into the trail as he tried to break his fall. His hand broke. His body tumbled with the bike. With each roll, bruises ensued. By the time he came to land just feet from the now agitated baboons, he had also dislocated his right wrist. As the baboons rose to take on a defensive stance, out of nowhere a car came down the road. The baboons retreated and went on their way.

The car came to a screeching halt beside the injured lad. The driver picked him up and took him to the local medical center for treatment. Another life-threatening moment in Levi's life strengthened his belief that a higher power had once again intervened on his behalf.

Author's Note

Hitting the tree alone could have been deadly at the speed my bike was traveling. But to then be hurled toward a group of Baboons with babies was definitely a testament of the power of Divine Intervention. The car came at just the exact moment to keep me from being savaged by the monkeys that surely would have pulled me limb from limb to protect their young.

God was there and stopped certain tragedy.

Story 9
Record Setting Tiger Fish on the Zambezi

From the time of his youth, Levi and his friends would trek to the cool clean waters of the Zambezi River to swim, explore and sit in the white sands of the shore. They loved to fish for tilapia, babel, trout and tiger fish.

The Zambezi River is the fourth largest river in Africa and is home to one of the continent's most sought-after fresh water game fish: the tiger fish. Sometimes called the "striped water dog," the tiger fish is an extremely aggressive predator that feeds on baitfish.

On a cool September morning Levi, his brother, and a group of friends set off to the Zambezi River for a day of fishing and fun.

The walk to the river was always long and hot. When they arrived the boys often cooled themselves at the river's edge. The lads all knew how to swim so they dove in and enjoyed water games, races and then began fishing. The group of boys had spent their entire childhoods hunting, fishing, and swimming together. They were like a large family of boys who enjoyed all things outdoors.

The morning was perfect for fishing. It was cool, and the sky was clear. They settled on a pristine stretch of river for tiger fishing. All along the river hippos, crocodiles and incredible wild birds rested, hunted, and cooled in the waters of the Zambezi.

This particular day was special. After having tea, the boys gathered at the river where they were met by river guides, Munyanya and his cousin Kashawindo. These men were part of generations of experts in the area. Their parents owned large wooden canoes which they used to guide anglers, novice and expert alike, for more than a decade. They had grown up fishing and taking others on fishing expeditions for many years.

The boys boarded a canoe with a canopy for shade. The guides provided fishing tackle for spinning and luring fish. This was not a typical fishing outing. This was serious. They were going to catch fish. There were rods and reels of all sorts and sizes. The boys were excited to get started.

As they puttered along in the canoe, their guide told them a little about the history of fishing on the Zambezi.

"Certainly, the tiger fish is the most fun to catch." Kashawindo explained. "But they can be challenging as well." Tiger fish are a member of the piranha family and have razor sharp teeth. They can grow to thirty inches in length and are noted for their strength and leaps out of the water when caught on a hook.

As the elderly gentleman paddled the canoe to a cove of rocks in the middle of the river, they noticed eagles flying above. Many were sitting regally on the branches of trees overhanging the river's edge. A herd of elephants emerged from the forest for a cool drink and shower in the river. Baby elephants rolled around in the muddy shoreline while their mothers kept a watchful eye. Crocodiles basked in the sun. As the canoes paddled by some would slam their tails in the water and submerge out of sight.

While fishing in the river is always good, the hotter months of September to November were always the best for tiger fish catching. This was the breeding season for the fish, causing them to be more active, feeding often, and hungrier than usual. The water level is lowest during the warm season, making visibility at its best.

The boys were given fishing gear to meet the seriousness of tiger fishing. Strong rods, medium action, with thick monofilament line. Excitedly the boys began casting clumsily. Eventually, with some simple instruction, the boys got the hang of it. They cast slightly upstream letting the lure sink. Over and over the boys hauled in tiger fish. Everyone except Levi. Disgruntled, he sighed. The other boys continued to haul in good sized fish. Levi had managed to snag three insignificant fish. He was discouraged. Levi was not about to give up, though. He cast his line again and again. Finally, a hit! A big hit! The tiger fish took off pulling line from the reel quickly. It leapt into the air.

"Don't allow any slack!" shouted his brother Kenny. "Keep on him until he is in the rocks!" Levi heard his friends shouting that he had a sure record breaker on the line. They cheered him on as he fought the fish this way and that. The mammoth fish surged and recoiled causing Levi to have to reel and release over and over. He did not want this monster fish to break his line. At only ten years old, and slightly built, Levi had his hands full with this massive fish.

The fish weaved in amongst the rocks attempting to dislodge the hook from its big mouth. Levi scrambled across the rocks, elevating his pole to keep the line tight. The fish was impressive. The boys yelled excitedly in encouragement. Several times the huge fish gave a mighty leap into the air and nearly pulled Levi into the water. The fish was finally landed on the rocks and Kenny grabbed it to secure it before it could flop itself back into the river. Levi stood up and took the great fish into his hands. It was huge! It was nearly thirty inches long and weighed in at sixty pounds. It was the largest tiger fish caught in the waters of the Zambezi.

The beautiful horizontal stripes and red tipped fins gave the tiger fish its name. Levi avoided the terrifying mouth full of razor-sharp teeth. He set the fish back onto the rocks awaiting assistance to haul it to the canoe. As he did the fish flipped and nearly made an escape into the water. Levi threw himself on the fish and wrapped his hand in a towel to protect himself from the gaping mouth of the monster.

The fish struggled beneath the weight of the boy. The crocodiles on the other side of the river began to show interest in all the activity. If Levi were to be dragged into the water by the fish, it would all be over.

Three members of the fishing team picked up the fish and moved off the rocky crag. Tiger fish are very aggressive when they are caught and will attempt to bite anything or anyone within reach. They put the big fish into the fish box and canoed back to the starting point of the excursion. Levi did not try to retrieve his hook until he returned home. To do so could have cost him his hand. He proudly accepted the accolades from family, friends, and neighbors as he showed off the record setting fish. The story would grow exponentially over the years, but what a story to tell. It was a great day, a great day indeed.

Author's Notes

By the grace of God all ended well. No one got hurt, drowned or were attacked by the crocodiles nor hippos. God is present in all we do. Whether we are in nature enjoying all His gifts, in town, or at home, He is ever there for us

Story 10
Churning Waters

It was a cool September morning and much like other mornings, Levi and his brother Kenny and a group of their friends decided to go exploring. It was quite a group of young boys who went on the trek to the water treatment station. This may not seem like much of an adventure, but to these boys, the mysteries within the pumping station and its working parts was beckoning.

The pumping station of the water treatment plant sat atop a hill. It was long and steep and required some stealth to get to the top. The boys loved the challenge of the getting up the hill. They loved to watch the workings of the machinery that pumped the water in and out, cleansing it and making it potable for human use.

The boys got on their bikes and headed to the station. The hill was so steep that pedaling up was impossible, so they dismounted and walked their bikes to the top. The adrenaline was flowing. Not only was the hike up the hill quite difficult, the water treatment station was strictly prohibited. For any young boy on and quest for adventure, this meant excitement for all the boys. Levi and his friends were not rabble rousers or bad kids. They just loved an adventure, and when the adventure included breaking a rule or two, they were in!

The water treatment plant hosted three silos where open water looked like large swimming pools. Two of the pools were relatively calm, but the third was exciting as it churned the water in a tight whirlpool. It sounded like the mighty Victoria Falls. How could a silo of water produce such immense energy and force? The boys were fascinated by the shear energy it takes to make that sound. If one has ever stood at the edge of the Victoria Falls in all her glory, the sound is an incredible roar of water rushing over the mountains edge. The treatment plant mimicked that roar of water. The only difference? This water was contained in cement silos. It was not the free-flowing waters of the mighty river coming to a drop off and crashing to the bottom of the falls. This was water churning inside a silo like a huge caldron.

On this particular day the overseer to the treatment center had gone to get the chemicals for treating the water. The boys took full advantage and made their way to the whirling waters contained in the bins.

The boys came to the gate of the compound. Much to their chagrin it was padlocked. The boys thought about attempting to climb the fence. Looking upward they realized the fence was secured with razor wire to keep intruders out. They moved along the fence line hoping to find a break in the wire. George and Tebuho took one try at scaling the fence. No good. Andrew and Steven had taken the younger lads along the fence line to see if there was any other entry. There was not. Levi and the other boys looked disappointed. Kenny, Levi's brother and the older boys stood in a circle and discussed the options. They turned around to face the group awaiting a solution.

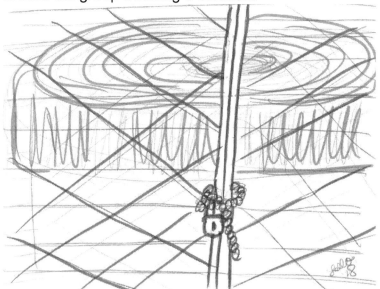

"There is no way in unless we break the locks on the gate." Andrew, one of the older boys, stated. "So, we have to decide if that is what we want to do." The boys looked from one to the other and back. Each one thought about the consequences versus the prize of being able to explore the mighty water treatment plant. One by one the boys nodded the affirmative. Once the boys had all agreed and pledged to never rat out the others, the conversation turned to the implementation of breaking the locks.

Lodo and Crispin thought the group might be able to pry the locks apart. The others shook their heads. The locks were nothing special, but they had nothing with which to pry them. The other boys looked around. The hill was laden with large rocks and stones. Kenny grabbed a rock and held it above his head.

"We have to smash the locks, and this is the only way I see to do it." The other boys cheered and grabbed rocks as well. There were three padlocks securing the gates and one by one the boys smashed them apart. They looked at each other as each lock fell to the ground. There was fear and excitement all around. If they got caught, it would surely be the worst punishment they could imagine. But if they didn't get caught, the adventure beyond the fence would be so great, that any way of getting there would be well worth it.

The boys, quite a large and conspicuous group, decided to go in two by two. Once inside the gates, they could span out and explore everything staying in a buddy system. All agreed and spread out as they entered the vast area.

The older boys easily hoisted themselves up onto the edges of the tanks to watch the massive waters swirling and rolling within. The younger boys had to be lifted to see into the vats. Levi, impatient to see into the basin, overestimated the effort and plunged headlong into the churning pool of water. His hand grasped the side of the barrel, but it was too much.

The current of the water ripped his hand free and thrust him into the choppy waters of the reservoir. Levi knew he was destined to be yet another drowning victim of the treatment plant. By providence, the older boys, dangling their legs into the churning water saw the events unfold. George and Steven saw Levi's legs as they passed by in a swirl of water. The boys each grabbed a leg and pulled hard against the suction of the whirlpool. They yelled orders to the other boys to try to save their friend.

"Grab his arm! Pull him up! Get his head above the water!" they scream excitedly. Kenny was holding Levi's leg with all his might. He knew if he let go his brother would be sucked into the turbine and he would be lost. Crispin lost his grip, yelling, "I can't hold it anymore." The rushing water was deafening as the boys fought to keep Levi from being sucked away. As each boy was exhausted into letting go, another would grab hold and yell more orders. "Hold on! Don't let go! We have to get him out!" they would yell over the water's thundering rush. Finally, after some minutes, and many relays from the boys trying to maintain a hold on Levi's arms and legs, he was miraculously pulled from the treacherous waters.

Gasping for air, he sputtered his thanks that his comrades had not given up. The boys learned a valuable lesson that day. The warning signs and locks they chose to ignore were there for a purpose. It was for their safety. They had heard stories of others who had lost their lives in the treatment plant but believed them to be only tales told to frighten them away. On this day they learned that the stories were true. The boys learned to respect signs and locks that kept them and others from danger.

This could have been the end of Levi's life, but God had other plans for him. Now when Levi reminisces about the events of that fateful day the scripture that comes to mind is Jeremiah 29:11 which states," For I know the thoughts that I think toward you, says the Lord, thoughts of peace and not of evil, to give you an expected end." It was not Levi's time to leave this earth. He was saved by the quick thinking and strength of his friends.

Author's Notes:

The encounter at the water plant was an extremely dangerous and life-threatening situation. Levi and his friends failed to obey the warning and prohibition signs at the water plant. If you find yourself in a situation like this, please get out. If you're told to not go in, you need not go in. The signs posted are there for your safety. Levi certainly hopes and prays that nobody has to experience nightmare of a self-inflicted near tragedy like the one described here.

Story 11
Exploring the Cave of Snakes

In the time of Levi's youth parents did not have to worry about their children in the way they do now. There was no fear of the children being snatched by terrorists or those in the human trafficking trade. The children spent most days outside playing. There were no computers and television was not a daytime addiction.

Levi and his friends spent all day from the wee hours of the morning until dusk outside exploring the rivers, woods, and caves near his family home.

Every day was a new adventure. Sometimes the boys would hunt for rabbits or birds. Other days it was a fishing adventure. And some days it was just exploration. Such was the day on a cool July morning when Levi, his brother Kenny, Regent, and several other friends decided to embark on a secret expedition to locate a hidden cave in the side of a hill.

The hills surrounding Zambia were steep and tall. There had been reports of hidden caves in the underbrush region and the boys were excited to try to find one. The boys knew it was going to be a long hike and an all-day venture, so they packed with them, Fanta soda, Canada Dry Ginger Ale, and some [6]chikoloki.

The cool July morning was perfect for the trek. They knew they may encounter elephants, lions, and other wildlife. The boys were on high alert.

Occasionally these explorations took many

---

[6] Chikoloki-A sugar water mixture used for boosting energy.

hours and the boys would be miles from home. So, for that eventuality they also carried with them tinned meat, breads, fruit, and rice. One of the boys carried a small pot which could be used to boil water for drinking and to cook the rice. Although to this point they had never gotten lost, it was a possibility. Therefore, coming fully prepared to stay in the hills overnight was paramount.

With slingshots for hunting and laden with the other goods for the day, the boys set off in a jubilant display of hoots and hollers. Along the way they successfully hunted two rabbits to add to their bounty.

The boys had learned early in their lives about the importance of hunting for the meat, not sport. They were also well schooled in field dressing their kills. Once the task was completed and the meat was salted for preservation and put in the basket, they continued on their way. As they climbed higher and higher the boys went in a serpentine back and forth on the hill looking for a break in the brush that would indicate a cave. Suddenly one of the boys yelled," Found it!" The others scrambled to the site. Sure enough, barely visible was a dark hole in the bushes.

The cavern was a large indent in the side of the hill with an entry just large enough for six or seven boys to sit comfortably inside. The floor was littered with rocks and small stones creating a semi clean space to set up camp. It had rained several days prior to their exploration and standing water was abundant. To the amazement of the crew there were small fish in the pools of clear water. Quite a find indeed.

Using small nets, they had carried with them, the boys snagged several small Barbell and Tilapia fish. With the fresh rabbit, fish and fruit this was a picnic fit for a king. The boys looked around for some dry wood to start the campfire. Once a good-sized bundle of wood was gathered a fire was started at the cave entrance. They had enough firewood to stay the entire day. The older boys set up a spit using long sticks to put the rabbit and fish over the fire. The smell of the drippings landing on the embers made the boys hungrier.

After [7]doing justice to the great bounty of food, the boys settled back to relax and enjoy the view far above the town. Some of the boys napped with tired legs and full bellies. The boys stirred some time later and gathered up the remaining food and the pot. It was dangerous to leave such things about as a lion or

---

[7] "Doing justice" to the food is a common phrase which means eating it with appreciation and gusto.

leopard could smell the meat and decide it was easy pickings.

With the change of breeze came a big stench. They tilted their heads high in the air to let the smell better enter their nostrils. What was that smell? The boys looked at each other as if to accuse one another of flatulence. They started laughing. But still, the smell did not dissipate.

It was much darker inside the cave, but that seemed to from where the stink was emanating. The odor was strong and pungent.

They talked briefly amongst themselves. Andrew piped up, "What if it's a lion?"

The other boys shook their heads. It was not likely that a lion was alone in a cave up the steep hill.

Lodo offered, "What about a Leopard? They like to be in trees and have been seen in the hills?" he offered

The boys again decided it was not a big cat in the cave. Levi sniffed the air again. The acrid odor seemed somehow familiar. It was a musk of sorts. Not unlike a skunk, only stronger. The older boys grabbed sticks which they wrapped dry grass around. They stuck the end with the grass into the fire and made torches. It was time to explore the cave and discover once and for all what was making that horrible smell.

As they slowly, step by step, eased inside the cave the smell intensified. The hairs on the back of the boys' neck stood on end. Their steps became slower and shorter. As the boys came to slight bend in the cave they raised their torches higher to try to see around the curve. There coiled up was a monster snake!

The boys halted suddenly causing the younger boys to plow into the backs of those carrying the light sticks. The snake, an [8]African Rock Python, was the largest they had ever seen. The boys stood mesmerized. The snake was every bit of eight feet long. Even coiled and resting the boys could tell it was the biggest snake any of them had ever seen. The boys sat quietly and observed the snake for some time. They were on high alert lest the snake move, but it seemed quite content being the subject of quiet contemplation and discussion.

The snake had a very large swell in its belly region signifying it had recently eaten something. The boys talked about the snake and what may have caused the stench.

---

[8] Python sebae natalensis

Kenny offered this explanation. "I bet we woke the snake with our fire and antics outside the cave entry. Since the snake was startled awake, he let off his musk. And because snakes don't like fire or people, he just stayed inside where he could digest his food." The other boys nodded in agreement.

Levi added, "I knew that smell was something I had experienced before. Remember when I saw the snake in the latrine?"

All the boys nodded affirmatively. Levi went on to regale the boys with the story of the massive Black Mamba that had almost had him for lunch. They listened, sometimes laughing, and sometimes being more serious. Snake business is always serious in Africa. When he was finished the boys chucked him on the shoulder and began to exit the cave. The snake remained still and quiet.

As the boys sat around the embers of their fire they reflected upon the day's event. Paul and Steven seemed the most shaken by the snake.

"Did you see the belly? That could have been a child." Paul offered. The boys thought about it. Kenny put that thought to rest.

"It was no doubt a small monkey. No way a child that small could come up this hill." Paul relaxed a bit. Then Steven looked sideways at the boys.

"Do you realize we could have been in real peril? What if that had been a Black Mamba or a Cobra in the cave? Those snakes don't like noise and are more aggressive." He shuddered as he shared his thoughts out loud. The boys all acknowledged the possibility. It was at that moment again Levi knew God was in control. The adventure to the cave could have turned into a tragedy. Instead each of the boys had a wonderful time and went home with a great tale to tell their families.

Author's Notes

This experience helped each of the boys identify the musky smell a snake gives off when threatened. Trips to the forests, hills, rivers and caves became safer because they learned a valuable survival skill.

God not only kept all the boys safe by providing the great snake with a meal before their arrival at the cave; He also gave them a take away that would prove very valuable in the years to come.

Story 12

To Grandmother's House We Go

Levi's father, Mr. Silas, was a no-nonsense, hard working man who made his living as a civil servant. He was honest and dependable. Mr. Silas loved his family and decided they were long overdue for a trip to see Levi's Paternal Grandmother in Mazabuka. The trip required taking the commercial bus from Katete to Lusaka and arriving in Mazabuka.

The ticket office of the bus line was to open at 8AM but a sign on the door let all travelers know it would be midday before ticket sales could happen. The bus leaving Katete was scheduled to leave at 2 PM but had to be rescheduled to 8 PM that evening due to maintenance issues. The many people waiting for the ticket office to open and to board the bus were growing weary as the day passed into evening.

Levi and his parents and siblings stood patiently in line when the ticket office finally opened for business. The line was long, and the children were fussy and tired. While in the line two men approached Levi's father as if to size him up. Deciding he was a pushover, they tried to cut in front of him. An argument between the three men ensued. Tembo and Mazala, the men trying to cut the line, were obviously intoxicated and indignant.

When the men could make no headway with Mr. Silas, they turned to Ms. Estelle and tried to bargain with her for a cut in the line. Ms. Estelle, who had been conversing with friends, politely walked away from the men. Mr. Silas saw the attempted exchange with his wife and became enraged. Mr. Silas was much taller and stronger than the men confronting his wife. He stepped up and gave a push to Tembo, who staggered into his compatriot and Mazala fell to the ground in a drunken haze. The two men then scuttled away to avoid further conflict.

Other men witnessing the incident came to Mr. Silas' aid. They surrounded the men and held them until a police officer arrived to arrest them. The two men were handcuffed and whisked away for disrupting the peace.

The day had turned to evening and the children were exhausted. Ms. Estelle lay a camp mattress on the ground for the children to sleep on while they maintained their place in line.

Levi's father, with tickets finally in hand, brought snacks for the children, as they awaited the coach buses arrival.

Levi's parents were engaged in conversation about upcoming vacations and plans for summer outings when suddenly SMACK!!! The ground seemed to shake under the loud noise of a rock hitting the ground near them.

Just moments before the attack, Levi had repositioned himself on the mattress on the ground. He had turned from his back to his side. There where he would have been laying was a large rock! The rock had been hurled from somewhere above. In the dark no one could tell exactly where it came from. But the intent was obvious. The rock was meant to punish and do as much damage a possible to the small child on the blanket.

Conjecture was that the rock was intended for Levi's father. Due to the massive weight of it, the rock fell short and fell on the bedding of the sleeping child.

A crowd gathered. Someone saw the culprits skulking away and noticed it was the two men who had been in the earlier altercation with Mr. Silas and Ms. Estelle. Evidently after questioning at the police station and believing it was just a drunken stupor that caused the men to act in such an impolite manner, the police discharged the men. They had returned for revenge.

The crowd of men stopped the perpetrators and after subduing them harshly awaited the police. Mr. Silas calmed the gathering crowd since no one was injured. A mob would have occurred had Mr. Silas not stepped up and quieted the angry group.

Once the men were arrested and taken into custody it was time to board the bus. Everyone would have a remarkable story to tell at grandmother's house. As for the men? They would now do real time in prison for their attempt to injure Mr. Silas and his family.

The bus trip was memorable and the visit with Levi's Grandmother was delightful. What could have been a tragedy ended in a wonderful memory for all to share in years to come.

Author's Notes

I see the hand of God over my life. If not for the Lord's protection, I would have lost my life on this day as well as many of the past experiences. God's hand protected me.

Author's Biography:

Levi Makala, PhD, DVM MBA
Born Livingstone Zambia, 1961

Levi H Makala was born in Zambia. His elementary, primary and secondary school years were spent in Livingstone and Canisius College, Chikuni, Zambia respectively.

He became a graduate student at the University of Zambia where he withdrew to take veterinary medicine and science in the USSR (Krasnodor, Russia and Kiev, Ukraine).

He obtained his Doctor of Veterinary Medicine (DVM) and Master of Veterinary Medicine and Science (MVSc) at the National Agricultural University of the Ukraine 1982-1988, PhD at the University of Bristol, Bristol, UK, 1993-1996 and MBA at Augusta University, Augusta, GA USA (2006-2009).

He was Assistant Director for research and Chief Veterinary Research officer at the Central Veterinary Research Institute, Balmoral, Zambia from 1996-2000, Visiting Professor at the National Research Center for Protozoan Diseases, Obihiro University, Hokkaido, Japan (2000-2003), and Scientist at Medical College of Georgia (Augusta University, Augusta GA USA, (2003-2018).

During these times Dr Makala conducted bench and clinical biomedical Science research, education and administration efforts in the areas of diabetes, infectious diseases, and blood disorders yielding universal reputation as a subject matter expert.

Dr. Levi Makala is an award-winning author of over 50 scientific publications in high impact factor internationally and nationally known and peer reviewed journals covering immunological aspects of infectious, auto immune diseases and blood disorders. He has also authored several book chapters for collegiate studies. He is recognized worldwide for ground-breaking contributions in the biomedical science community and sits on various steering and scientific peer-review committees.

Dr Makala has been called upon for multiple international national keynote speaking appearances. He is an active member at New Heights Community Church where he plays guitar in the praise and worship team and leads an adult bible study class.

Dr. Levi Makala reminisces what childhood was like growing up in sub-Saharan southern Africa, Zambia, the land of the mighty Victoria Falls. He opens up about what his life and experiences were like when he was young. This book captures the activities which fascinated and captivated him most when he was little, and his remarkable childhood experiences.

Here in the pages of this book, Levi explores experiences that caused smiles or even laughter, including those that brought back bitter memories in a lively and realistic way to cement his faith in a living God who sustained him throughout it all.

Dr Levi loves writing children's books. He feels as though he is going back in time and writing his own history every time he sits down to write to younger readers.

It is hoped that his childhood experiences will encourage the little ones to have perspective when they are navigating life. They should know that they are not alone but in the hands of an Almighty God. God knows each one of us before we are born, and He has good plans for all of us, if we choose Him.

Jeremiah 1: 5
"Before I formed you in the womb, I knew you, before you were born I set you apart; I appointed you as a prophet to the nations."
Jeremiah 29:11
For I know the plans I have for you," declares the LORD, "plans to prosper you and not to harm you, plans to give you hope and a future.

Accomplishments

Schools: Canisius College, Chikuni, Zambia; University of Zambia, National Agricultural University of the Ukraine, University of Bristol, Bristol, UK, Augusta University, Augusta, GA USA

Work: Zambian Government, Ministry of Agriculture and Livestock services (CVRI); National Research Center for Protozoan Diseases, Obihiro University, Hokkaido, Japan, Medical College of Georgia (Augusta University, Augusta GA

Jobs: Veterinary Surgeon, Principal Veterinary Research Officer, Director of Veterinary Research, Scientist, Visiting Professor, Educator, Entrepreneur, Author

40268843R00062

Made in the USA
Columbia, SC
12 December 2018